Extreme Downhill Skiing Moves

By Mary Firestone

Consultant:
John Pomeroy
Sport Manager
Canadian Freestyle Ski Association
Ottawa, Canada

CAPSTONE
HIGH-INTEREST
BOOKS

an imprint of Capstone Press
Mankato, Minnesota

Capstone High-Interest Books are published by Capstone Press
151 Good Counsel Drive, P.O. Box 669, Mankato, Minnesota 56002
http://www.capstone-press.com

Library of Congress Cataloging-in-Publication Data
Firestone, Mary.
    Extreme downhill skiing moves / by Mary Firestone.
    p. cm.—(Behind the moves)
    Summary: Discusses the sport of extreme downhill skiing, including the
unique equipment, safety measures, and aerial stunts.
    Includes bibliographical references (p. 31) and index.
    ISBN 0-7368-2153-8 (hardcover)
    1. Skis and skiing—Juvenile literature. 2. Extreme sports—Juvenile literature.
[1. Skis and skiing. 2. Extreme sports.] I. Title. II. Series.
GV854.315.F57 2004
796.93—dc21   2002155525

Editorial Credits

James Anderson, editor; Jason Knudson, book designer; Jo Miller, photo
    researcher; Karen Risch, product planning editor

Photo Credits

Corbis/Karl Weatherly, 10; David Stoecklien, 14
Getty Images/Al Bello, 4, 16; Mike Powell, 7; Clive Brunskill, 18; Jamie Squire,
    23 (left), 25; Steven E. Frischling/Brattleboro Reformer, 23 (right)
PhotoDisc, Inc., 4 (inset), 10 (inset), 18 (inset), 26 (inset)
SportsChrome-USA, 13, 20, 21 29; Mountain Stock/Chaco Mohler, cover, 8;
    Hank de Vre/Mountain Stock, 12, 26

1 2 3 4 5 6 08 07 06 05 04 03

Table of Contents

Jonny Moseley does a dinner roll.

Learn about:

■ *Freeskiing*

■ *Freestyle skiing*

■ *History*

Chapter One

Extreme Downhill Skiing

After Jonny Moseley won the gold medal in moguls skiing at the 1998 Winter Olympics, he took some time off. He taught young skiers how to perform the tricks he learned. He also taught himself a new trick called the dinner roll. This trick is two off-centered spins.

Moseley decided to try this new trick at the 2002 Olympics in Salt Lake City, Utah. He landed the dinner roll. His trick was the most difficult ever done in the moguls event at the Olympic Games. But his score was not high enough to win a medal.

Freeskiing is a new challenge for Jonny Moseley now. He skis on steep, high mountain slopes. When possible, he leaps off natural jumps such as cliffs. He uses his skills to find new ways to express himself on the slopes.

Types of Extreme Downhill Skiing

Extreme downhill skiing is a sport for expert skiers. Freeskiers perform stunts and go for huge jumps, sometimes off cliffs. Some freeskiers ride helicopters to steep mountains and ski down.

Very few skiers take part in freeskiing. These skiers risk their lives if they make one wrong move.

Aerial skiing and big air are also forms of extreme downhill skiing. These types of skiing are called freestyle skiing.

Freestyle skiers perform backflips, somersaults, and spins as they fly off ramps and jumps. Freestyle skiing takes place on designated slopes, often at competitive events.

History of Skiing

Ancient stone carvings in Norway show hunters using runners. These pieces of wood were shaped like skis. Runners helped early hunters move over snow to catch animals. Over time, runners became known as skis. People began using skis for cross-country travel. Soon, they began skiing for fun.

Skiing downhill became known as alpine skiing. Early alpine skiers used mountain climbing equipment to get up steep or rough mountain slopes.

Ski lifts were invented in the 1920s. The lifts meant skiers no longer needed to hike up mountains. The slopes near the ski lifts were sometimes overused. The snow on the slopes became packed down.

Some skiers ride helicopters to mountain tops

Extreme skiers do tricks off steep cliffs.

Skiers wanted the challenge of fresh snow again. Some skiers started to ski off-piste (PEEST). These people skied off the regular trails near ski lifts.

In 1949, Warren Miller began to make films that showed skiers on mountain slopes. His films helped introduce extreme downhill skiing to the world. Miller and others have helped make downhill skiing popular today.

Olympic skier Stein Ericksen was the first to perform a flip off a small jump in competition. By the 1970s, extreme ski events were common at ski resorts. In the 1980s, freestyle skiing was recognized by the International Ski Federation. Freestyle ski events are now a part of the Winter Olympic Games.

Skiers look for deep powder in bowls.

Learn about:

"Pow"

Cliff jumping

Traversing

Extreme Freeskiing Moves

Skiers begin freeski rides above the tree line. The tree line is where trees stop growing high on a mountain. The high altitudes and low oxygen levels create dry, deep powder snow.

Deep Powder

Deep powder is the best snow for skiing. It is not icy or slippery. Skiers can control their moves best in deep powder. A single snowfall can produce powder that is 6 feet (1.8 meters) deep. The deepest powder snow is found in bowls. These big valleys are on mountainsides.

Freeskiers call deep powder in bowls "pow." This deep powder snow slows a skier down because skis sink in the snow. A skier must lean back to stop the skis from sinking.

Cliff Jumping and Chute Riding

Freeskiers use cliffs and jumps to "go big." They ski down the steepest slopes or drop off cliffs. Going big over a cliff is also called "hucking." Before they jump, skiers always check the landings at the bottom of a cliff. The area must be clear of trees and rocks.

Cliff jumping is a dangerous part of freeskiing.

Freeskiers also ski down chutes. These narrow patches of snow and ice are between long areas of rock. Chutes are dangerous. Some chutes are almost straight up and down.

Chutes are steep and narrow.

Jump Turns

To perform jump turns, skiers extend their bodies while turning their skis. The skier's upper body must remain still and centered over the skis. Only the legs and arms move. Skiers float over the snow as they move their skis from left to right.

Skiers create "sluff."

Getting Down the Mountain

Freeskiers often release lightly packed snow called "sluff." This snow was once on the ground but is kicked up as a skier passes over it. Sluff can make skiers appear to be riding in a cloud of white smoke.

Skiers sometimes traverse the side of a mountain if the powder is too heavy. These skiers move sideways instead of straight down a hill.

To traverse, a skier must always have more weight on the downhill ski to avoid falling. The upper body must stay centered over the skis. Traversing helps skiers avoid being buried by loose snow that might slide down a mountain.

The fall line is the natural route down a mountain. If a ball or a rock naturally rolled down a mountain, gravity would pull it down a certain path. Skiers try to move down the fall line. Good skiers can feel gravity pull them. They can sense the fall line as they move down a mountain.

Extreme Downhill Skiing Slang

crater—to make a big hole in the snow after a big air

going big—flying high off cliffs or jumps

hucking—to fly off a big cliff

sluff—the snow kicked up by skiers as they go down a mountain

star fish—to fall and tumble down a hill, with legs and arms spread out

tweak out—to pull a grab back or to one side

yard sale—to crash and leave equipment scattered on the ground

Moguls is a popular Olympic event.

Learn about:

- **Olympic events**
- **Big air**
- **Inverted tricks**

Chapter Three

Extreme Freestyle Moves

Freestyle skiing is more widely accepted than freeskiing. Freestyle skiing is currently the only extreme downhill skiing in the Olympics. Freestyle events in the Olympics are the moguls and aerials. Big air events are done at professional competitions but not at the Olympics. During these events, skiers jump high in the air to perform tricks.

Moguls

In freestyle moguls, skiers race downhill over bumps called moguls. They perform tricks off two 8-foot (2.4-meter) jumps. These jumps are usually placed one-third and two-thirds of the way down the course.

Moguls runs can last less than 30 seconds.

Skiing over moguls is difficult. Moguls skiers bend their knees to lessen the weight on their skis. They use their poles to keep their balance. Then, they turn their skis in the next direction.

Moguls skiers are judged on how they turn through the moguls. Judges also rate the difficulty of the "airs" or tricks performed. A mogul course is usually 721 feet (220 meters) long. A skier can finish the course in less than 30 seconds.

Aerials

In aerials, skiers jump off steep ramps called kickers. These skiers fly up to 50 feet (15 meters) in the air. They perform tricks while in the air. Aerial skiers can do more twists and flips in the air than athletes in any other sport.

Skiers do aerial tricks off a kicker.

Big Air

Skiers add personal style to tricks during big air competitions. In these events, skiers launch from a ramp into the air and perform tricks.

Big air jumps and landings are less steep than in aerials events. These jumps and landings allow skiers to face backward as they take off or land.

Big air events are becoming more popular at competitions. Big air may one day be in the Olympics.

Extreme Tricks

Aerial and big air skiers perform many tricks. To do an iron cross, a skier crosses the tip of one ski over the other, behind the back. During the backscratcher, both skis are pulled up behind the skier's back. A helicopter is a 360-degree vertical spin.

When skiers are inverted, they are upside down. During an inverted helicopter, an upside down skier spins in the air. The skis look like the blades of a helicopter.

An iron cross is done during big air events.

Inverted Helicopter

Grabs

Experienced skiers also perform grabs during their moves. Skiers lift their skis toward their body and grab the skis.

Skiers do several types of grabs. These include the Indy grab and the mute grab. Skiers do an Indy grab when they grab the left ski with the left hand near the boot.

A mute grab is a modified iron cross. A skier grabs the right ski with the left hand, or the left ski with the right hand. Next, the skier crosses the grabbed ski over the other ski. Mute grabs are made in front of the binding.

Skiers lift their skis when performing grabs.

Freeskiing can be a dangerous sport.

Learn about:

- **Avalanches**
- **Flat light**
- **Gear**

Chapter Four

Safety

Skiing can be dangerous. Even the best skiers are at risk of being hurt or killed in avalanches. An avalanche is a large amount of snow or ice that suddenly moves down a mountain side.

Freeskiers should call the nearest ranger station before they make a run. When the conditions are right for skiing, skiers should let the rangers know when and where they will be skiing.

Avalanche Equipment

Freeskiers sometimes wear backpacks when they ski. The backpacks contain a shovel, a probe, and an avalanche beacon. Skiers can use these tools if they are buried under snow. Skiers can also use this equipment to help others buried in avalanches.

A probe is a collapsible metal stick that is 10 feet (3 meters) long when it is extended. Skiers use probes to find other skiers who have been lost in an avalanche.

An avalanche beacon is like a walkie-talkie. It can receive and send signals. Skiers who have fallen can use a beacon to call for help.

Flat Light

Skiers try to ski on sunny days to avoid "flat light." This happens when white snow and a white, cloudy sky look the same.

Flat light makes it hard for a skier to know if the snow ahead is getting steeper or flattening out. Skiers should never go too fast during flat light conditions.

Clothing

Skiers wear goggles that block harmful rays of the sun. The glare from the sun on snow can keep a skier from seeing properly.

Some freestyle skiers wear helmets. Helmets worn in freestyle competitions are different from helmets worn by casual skiers. Competition helmets are thicker and have more padding.

For cold weather, skiers dress in layers. Layers are necessary if a skier gets warm. If skiers get too warm, layers can be removed. A skier's sweat can cause chills. A chill can lead to hypothermia. This deadly condition occurs when a person's body temperature is lower than normal.

The best skiers spend years practicing. They understand that to enjoy their sport, they must first be familiar with basic moves.

Skiers carry safety equipment in their backpacks.

Words to Know

avalanche (AV-uh-lanch)—a large mass of snow, ice, or earth that suddenly moves down the side of a mountain

chute (SHOOT)—a narrow rock pathway with snow and ice at the center

fall line (FAWL LINE)—the natural route down a mountain

flat light (FLAT LITE)—the light on cloudy days that makes it difficult for skiers to see

hypothermia (hye-puh-THUR-mee-uh)—a condition that occurs when a person's body temperature falls several degrees below normal

piste (PEEST)—an overused trail

tree line (TREE LINE)—the point where trees on a mountain stop growing due to lack of oxygen, short growing seasons, and poor soil

To Learn More

Pollack, Pamela. *Ski: Your Guide to Jumping, Racing, Skiboarding, Nordic, Backcountry, Aerobatics, and More.* Extreme Sports. Washington D.C.: National Geographic Society, 2002.

Tomlinson, Joe. *Extreme Sports: The Illustrated Guide to Maximum Adrenaline Thrills.* New York: Carlton Books, 2002.

Young, Ian. *X Games: Action Sports Grab the Spotlight.* High Five Reading. Mankato, Minn.: Capstone Curriculum Publishing, 2002.

Useful Addresses

Canadian Freestyle Ski Association
Suite 305
2197 Riverside Drive
Ottawa, ON K1H 7X3
Canada

International Free Skiers Association
P.O. Box 682673
Park City, UT 84068

Internet Sites

Do you want to find out more about extreme downhill skiing?
Let FactHound, our fact-finding hound dog, do the research for you.

Here's how:

1) Visit *http://www.facthound.com*
2) Type in the **Book ID** number: **0736821538**
3) Click on **FETCH IT**.

FactHound will fetch Internet sites picked by our editors just for you!

Index